Daily Quotes

for

Daily Blessings

Words to Get You Where You Need to Be

Dr. Jamie T. Pleasant; Ph.D.

Daily Quotes

for

Daily Blessings

Words to Get You Where You Need to Be

Dr. Jamie T. Pleasant; Ph.D.

Daily Quotes for Daily Blessings: Words to Get you Where You Need to Be

Copyright © 2014 by Dr. Jamie T. Pleasant; Ph.D.

Biblion Publishing LLC

All rights reserved. No portion of this book may be reproduced, stored in a retrieval system or transmitted in any form or by any means — electronic, mechanical, photocopy, recording or other without the prior written authorization of the author — except for a brief quotation in printed reviews.

First Edition / First Printing

ISBN-978-1-940698-04-5

Daily Quotes for Daily Blessings

Are you ready to go to the next level in your life? Do you want to walk in your destiny? Are you tired of living each day not really knowing whether you are in purpose or not? If you answered yes to any of these questions, this book is for you! "Daily Quotes for Daily Blessings" will take you on a journey to uncovering your uniqueness. Each quote presents a personal note to help you reach new heights in your life! You will learn new ways to stay motivated and inspired. You will walk in a newness of confidence and joy. Get ready to be blessed beyond your wildest imagination.

Dedication

To my daddy, Anthony T. Pleasant, who was a perfect example to me of a real man. To my wife Kimberly (oh, how I love you darling!), my two sons; Christian and Zion, and daughter, Nacara.

To my New Zion Christian Church Family, Clark Atlanta University, Mr. Harril and Hattie Sanders (you were great surrogate parents to me during my teenage years) and Charles and Joyce Williams.

Humbly Yours in Christ,

Apostle Jamie T. Pleasant

Getting the most out of "Daily Quotes for Daily Blessings"

Congratulations on purchasing this book! Get ready to take your life to a new level. This book contains many inspiring notes of encouragement to inspire you to accomplish all that you are destined to walk in. You can use this book for personal growth or group study sessions. Sit back and relax as you read these inspiring notes.

> **Success will not come in one night, but one night success will come.**

Daily Quotes for Daily Blessings

Your thoughts

_____

_____

_____

_____

_____

_____

_____

_____

_____

_____

_____

Daily Quotes for Daily Blessings

> **You can't share your 8X10 vision with someone that has a 4X6 mind.**

Daily Quotes for Daily Blessings

Your thoughts

_____

_____

_____

_____

_____

_____

_____

_____

_____

> **Sometimes you must distance yourself from the crowd to get closer to your dream.**

Daily Quotes for Daily Blessings

Your thoughts

Successful people will always find a way, when other people can only find excuses.

Daily Quotes for Daily Blessings

Your thoughts

_____

_____

_____

_____

_____

_____

_____

_____

_____

_____

Daily Quotes for Daily Blessings

> **The best time to change is before you have to!**

Daily Quotes for Daily Blessings

Your thoughts

_____

_____

_____

_____

_____

_____

_____

_____

_____

_____

> **The best way to deal with those that are weighing you down with their ISSUES, is to UNSUBSCRIBE to their friendship.**

Daily Quotes for Daily Blessings

Your thoughts

> **Great leadership is not measured by the number of followers one has, but by the number of leaders one has developed.**

Daily Quotes for Daily Blessings

Your thoughts

Don't let bad thoughts <u>INCH</u> into your mind, they will soon become a <u>RULER</u> of your life.

Daily Quotes for Daily Blessings

Your thoughts

> **Work like the check you want, not like the check you got.**

Daily Quotes for Daily Blessings

Your thoughts

> **The faith walk is more difficult than the faith talk.**

Daily Quotes for Daily Blessings

Your thoughts

_____

_____

_____

_____

_____

_____

_____

_____

_____

The world has enough self-starters and not enough self-finishers.

Daily Quotes for Daily Blessings

Your thoughts

You must love yourself before you can love others!

Daily Quotes for Daily Blessings

Your thoughts

_____

_____

_____

_____

_____

_____

_____

_____

_____

_____

_____

> **A problem that is well defined, is already more than half solved.**

Daily Quotes for Daily Blessings

Your thoughts

Why are you waiting on your future when your future is waiting on you?

Daily Quotes for Daily Blessings

Your thoughts

> **New thoughts poured into old minds will only leak into a bucket full of frustration.**

Daily Quotes for Daily Blessings

Your thoughts

Don't follow your dreams, catch up with them and live.

Daily Quotes for Daily Blessings

Your thoughts

> **Opportunity is always knocking, but nothing will happen if you don't get up and open the door.**

Daily Quotes for Daily Blessings

Your thoughts

> **Opportunity is knocking at your door. Can you handle the knock?**

Daily Quotes for Daily Blessings

Your thoughts

> **Don't wait on your moment, your moment is waiting on you.**

Daily Quotes for Daily Blessings

Your thoughts

_____

_____

_____

_____

_____

_____

_____

_____

_____

_____

> **People that pray, don't worry. People that worry, don't pray.**

Daily Quotes for Daily Blessings

Your thoughts

_____

_____

_____

_____

_____

_____

_____

_____

_____

_____

> **It's hard for people to bring you down when you stay prayed up.**

Daily Quotes for Daily Blessings

Your thoughts

> **Life can be full of problems; living is knowing how to not let them negatively affect you.**

Daily Quotes for Daily Blessings

Your thoughts

> **Don't try to be anyone different, you already are.**

Daily Quotes for Daily Blessings

Your thoughts

> **Don't fall in love, walk in it. The journey is a lot better.**

Daily Quotes for Daily Blessings

Your thoughts

Daily Quotes for Daily Blessings

> **Following your dreams doesn't mean you get to go back to sleep.**

Daily Quotes for Daily Blessings

Your thoughts

_____

_____

_____

_____

_____

_____

_____

_____

_____

_____

> **It's never too late to become who you could have been.**

Daily Quotes for Daily Blessings

Your thoughts

Some people are so negative that if you put them in a dark room, they will automatically start developing.

Daily Quotes for Daily Blessings

Your thoughts

The best way to get rid of negative people is to start saying something positive.

Daily Quotes for Daily Blessings

Your thoughts

Don't become limited by your challenges, challenge your limits.

Daily Quotes for Daily Blessings

Your thoughts

> **Stop chasing after the wrong things so right things can catch up to you.**

Daily Quotes for Daily Blessings

Your thoughts

Don't share your permanent plans with temporary people.

Daily Quotes for Daily Blessings

Your thoughts

_____

_____

_____

_____

_____

_____

_____

_____

_____

_____

> **I'm not all that I want to be, but thank God, I'm not at all what I used to be.**

Daily Quotes for Daily Blessings

Your thoughts

> **If you try to live up to the approval of others, you will die by their constant criticism.**

Daily Quotes for Daily Blessings

Your thoughts

As a man thinketh, prayeth and doeth, so is he.

Daily Quotes for Daily Blessings

Your thoughts

> **You can't be framed if you're not in the picture.**

Daily Quotes for Daily Blessings

Your thoughts

Follow your heart, but carry a sound mind with you!

Daily Quotes for Daily Blessings

Your thoughts

Don't measure a person's success on what they have, but on what they have done, with what they have.

Daily Quotes for Daily Blessings

Your thoughts

Friendships are like x-rays. You won't know if they are positive or negative until they see the darkest areas of your life exposed.

Daily Quotes for Daily Blessings

Your thoughts

> **You will never have a six-figure income if you possess a five-figure mind.**

Daily Quotes for Daily Blessings

Your thoughts

_____

_____

_____

_____

_____

_____

_____

_____

_____

_____

_____

> **If you aim for nothing, you will definitely hit it.**

Daily Quotes for Daily Blessings

Your thoughts

> **Empty your hands of your negative past so you can embrace the things of your positive future.**

Daily Quotes for Daily Blessings

Your thoughts

Many are standing in the need of prayer because few fall on their knees to get the power that comes from prayer.

Daily Quotes for Daily Blessings

Your thoughts

> **The secret in life is not getting what you want, but wanting it after you get it.**

Daily Quotes for Daily Blessings

Your thoughts

> **Choose friends that want what you want, not those that want to take what you got.**

Daily Quotes for Daily Blessings

Your thoughts

> **The grass always looks greener on the other side until you cross over and see how much it costs to keep it looking that way.**

Daily Quotes for Daily Blessings

Your thoughts

Don't hesitate to subtract those out of your life that are not adding to it.

Daily Quotes for Daily Blessings

Your thoughts

> **You can't go up in life if you are constantly looking down on yourself.**

Daily Quotes for Daily Blessings

Your thoughts

> **It is not about what someone can bring to the table, but how much that person can expand it.**

Daily Quotes for Daily Blessings

Your thoughts

> **Be watchful of those that constantly remind you of your imperfections without ever acknowledging theirs.**

Daily Quotes for Daily Blessings

Your thoughts

> **A first class woman doesn't deserve a last class man and vice versa.**

Daily Quotes for Daily Blessings

Your thoughts

Everyone has baggage. You need someone that is willing to help you unpack as you are willing to help them do the same.

Daily Quotes for Daily Blessings

Your thoughts

> **When what's possible, no longer seems probable, expect the impossible.**

Daily Quotes for Daily Blessings

Your thoughts

Do something you've never done, and you'll get something you've never got.

Daily Quotes for Daily Blessings

Your thoughts

Don't let a momentary thrill become a permanent problem in your life!

Daily Quotes for Daily Blessings

Your thoughts

___

You're not done if it didn't work out, but you are finished if you quit.

Daily Quotes for Daily Blessings

Your thoughts

God is good all the time and even when times aren't good.

Daily Quotes for Daily Blessings

Your thoughts

Gifts and talents can get you there, but only God's grace can keep you there!

Daily Quotes for Daily Blessings

Your thoughts

> **I would rather be used by God than blessed by the devil.**

Daily Quotes for Daily Blessings

Your thoughts

_____

_____

_____

_____

_____

_____

_____

_____

_____

_____

Daily Quotes for Daily Blessings

> **When people throw stones at you, build something positive out of it.**

Daily Quotes for Daily Blessings

Your thoughts

> **When you are hurt, go ahead and cry a river of tears, then build a bridge and get over it.**

Daily Quotes for Daily Blessings

Your thoughts

Daily Quotes for Daily Blessings

> **No one will ever be as excited about you, than you!**

Daily Quotes for Daily Blessings

Your thoughts

_____

_____

_____

_____

_____

_____

_____

_____

_____

_____

When you think with your head, it causes you to dream. When you feel with your heart, it causes you to act. When you act with your hands, it causes you to be.

Daily Quotes for Daily Blessings

Your thoughts

_____

_____

_____

_____

_____

_____

_____

_____

_____

_____

> **Your reality becomes what you focus on and what you focus on, becomes your reality.**

Daily Quotes for Daily Blessings

Your thoughts

> **Change the way you see things, and a change will take place in the things you see.**

Daily Quotes for Daily Blessings

Your thoughts

If life deals you a bad hand, don't quit, reshuffle the deck.

Daily Quotes for Daily Blessings

Your thoughts

> **You have to kneel very low in your prayer life to stand very tall in your real life.**

Daily Quotes for Daily Blessings

Your thoughts

> **Always pray for what you want, but never forget to thank Him for what you get!**

Daily Quotes for Daily Blessings

Your thoughts

_____

_____

_____

_____

_____

_____

_____

_____

_____

_____

_____

> **People will always expect more of you than what they expect of themselves.**

Daily Quotes for Daily Blessings

Your thoughts

> **The secret in getting <u>AHEAD</u> lies with the action of getting off your <u>BEHIND!</u>**

Daily Quotes for Daily Blessings

Your thoughts

_____

_____

_____

_____

_____

_____

_____

_____

_____

_____

> **Money shouldn't motivate you; it should be a result of your motivation.**

Daily Quotes for Daily Blessings

Your thoughts

_____

_____

_____

_____

_____

_____

_____

_____

_____

> **If you give a man a fish, you will feed him for a day. If you teach him how to fish, you will feed him for a lifetime. If you teach him how to buy the lake, he can get others to do the fishing for him.**

Daily Quotes for Daily Blessings

Your thoughts

> **Reach deep down inside yourself and find your greatness. Then, reach deeper inside and pull it out.**

Daily Quotes for Daily Blessings

Your thoughts

There is a miracle on the inside of you!

Daily Quotes for Daily Blessings

Your thoughts

A dream without a plan of action is just a hallucination.

Daily Quotes for Daily Blessings

Your thoughts

In order to go where you have never gone, you must do what you have never done.

Daily Quotes for Daily Blessings

Your thoughts

> **Before you put someone in their place, make sure you are properly seated in yours.**

Daily Quotes for Daily Blessings

Your thoughts

You can't get a piece of peace until you allow God to be the slice of your life.

Daily Quotes for Daily Blessings

Your thoughts

_____

_____

_____

_____

_____

_____

_____

_____

_____

_____

_____

> **You can't become who you are destined to be, by staying where you are.**

Daily Quotes for Daily Blessings

Your thoughts

> **You are seeking God because He is pursuing you!**

Daily Quotes for Daily Blessings

Your thoughts

> **If you think you can, you will. If you think you can't, you won't.**

Daily Quotes for Daily Blessings

Your thoughts

_____

_____

_____

_____

_____

_____

_____

_____

_____

_____

> **You can't give good advice to someone with a bad understanding!**

Daily Quotes for Daily Blessings

Your thoughts

> **A dream is just a spiritual event that wants to be birthed in the natural realm.**

Daily Quotes for Daily Blessings

Your thoughts

> **Don't look back; look forward, that's where your blessings are!**

Daily Quotes for Daily Blessings

Your thoughts

If you look up, you'll get up and then you can stay up.

Daily Quotes for Daily Blessings

Your thoughts

_____

_____

_____

_____

_____

_____

_____

_____

_____

_____

If you pray LONG and STRONG, You won't go WRONG!

Daily Quotes for Daily Blessings

Your thoughts

You can't walk in your future until you leave your past behind.

Daily Quotes for Daily Blessings

Your thoughts

> **There are two things in life that are constant; change and more change.**

Daily Quotes for Daily Blessings

Your thoughts

> **You are not a body that has a spirit; you are a spirit that has a body.**

Daily Quotes for Daily Blessings

Your thoughts

> **If you focus on the eternal blessings of God, your temporary problems will fade away.**

Daily Quotes for Daily Blessings

Your thoughts

God will do, what only He can do, that you can't do, when you trust Him.

Daily Quotes for Daily Blessings

Your thoughts

> **It might take you many years to become an overnight success. Don't quit!**

Daily Quotes for Daily Blessings

Your thoughts

> **If you don't know where you are going, you will definitely get there.**

Daily Quotes for Daily Blessings

Your thoughts

_____

_____

_____

_____

_____

_____

_____

_____

_____

_____

> **When you become a know it all, that is all you will ever know.**

Daily Quotes for Daily Blessings

Your thoughts

_____

_____

_____

_____

_____

_____

_____

_____

_____

_____

Think while you are inside of the box on ways to get out of it.

Daily Quotes for Daily Blessings

Your thoughts

_____

_____

_____

_____

_____

_____

_____

_____

_____

_____

Joy is not found in the position you hold over others in life, but the life you bring to others in whatever position you hold.

Daily Quotes for Daily Blessings

Your thoughts

_____

_____

_____

_____

_____

_____

_____

_____

_____

_____

> **We never pray the way we should pray until we have to pray.**

Daily Quotes for Daily Blessings

Your thoughts

_____

_____

_____

_____

_____

_____

_____

_____

_____

_____

Sometimes your biggest obstacle is right in front of you in the mirror.

Daily Quotes for Daily Blessings

Your thoughts

> **Mangers make sure things are done right. Leaders always do the right thing.**

Daily Quotes for Daily Blessings

Your thoughts

> **If you knew then, what you know now, it wouldn't be then, it would still be now.**

Daily Quotes for Daily Blessings

Your thoughts

You must learn what you've never learned to earn what you've never earned.

Daily Quotes for Daily Blessings

Your thoughts

_____

_____

_____

_____

_____

_____

_____

_____

_____

_____

Epilogue

One of the best ways to get where you need to be in your life is for you to give your life to Christ Jesus. Repeat these simple words and it will be a done deal. Repeat the following: Lord Christ Jesus as of this very moment, I accept you as Lord and Savior of my life. I now give my life to you to be fashioned for your purpose and glory. Lord, all of these things that I have said, I truly believe in my heart and have confessed with my mouth to you. I know now that I have received everlasting life based on the work that Christ has done and will continue to do in my life. Lord Christ, thank you for bringing me to this point of my life where I surrender my all to you. It is in the Holy Spirit through Christ Jesus, I say Amen.

Humbly Yours in Christ

Apostle Jamie T. Pleasant

Epilogue

Book Dr. Pleasant

Book Dr. Pleasant for a Speaking Engagement

For speaking engagements, please contact Dr. Jamie T. Pleasant at admin@newzionchristianchurch.org or 678.845.7055

These books can be purchased at any bookstore or online at amazon.com, barnesandnoble.com and many other stores and outlets.

Book Dr. Pleasant

About the Author

About the Author

Dr. Jamie T. Pleasant; Ph.D. is a tenured marketing professor at Clark Atlanta University, which is an AACSB accredited institution of higher learning. AACSB accreditation is the highest and most distinguished accredited affiliation of business schools around the entire world. He is also the Chief Executive Pastor and Founder of New Zion Christian Church in Suwanee, Georgia. As a modern day polymath, he holds a bachelor's degree in Physics from Benedict College in Columbia, South Carolina, Marketing Studies from Clemson University and an M.B.A. in Marketing from Clark Atlanta University. On August 13, 1999, Apostle Pleasant achieved a Georgia Tech milestone by becoming the first African American to graduate with a Ph.D. in Business Management in the school's 120 plus year history.

About the Author

God gave him the vision to establish a Biblically based economic development initiative for New Zion Christian Church. He remains at the pulse of the economic business sector. As a result, Apostle Pleasant is in constant demand to train, speak and teach others at all levels in ministries and the private sector about business and economic development across the country. He has created cutting edge and industry leading ministerial programs in the church such as The Financial Literacy Academy For Youth (FLAFY), where youth from the ages of 13-19 attend 12 week intense classes on financial money management principles. At the end of 12 weeks, they receive a "Personal Finance" certificate of achievement. Other ministries he has pioneered include; The Wealth Builders Investment Club (WBIC), which educates and allows members to actively invest in the stock market, along with the much celebrated Institute of Entrepreneurship (IOE), where participants earn a certificate in

About the Author

Entrepreneurship after three months of comprehensive training in all aspects of starting and owning a successful competitive business. The main goal and purpose of IOE is that each year one of the trained businesses will be awarded up to $10,000 start up money to ensure financial success. The newly added SAT & PSAT prep courses for children ages 9-19 fuels the potential success of all who walk through the doors of New Zion Christian Church.

Apostle Pleasant has met with political officials such as President Clinton and Nelson Mandela. He has delivered the opening prayer for the born again Christian and comedian, Steve Harvey. He has performed marriage ceremonies and counseled numerous celebrated personalities such as Usher Raymond (Confessions Recording Artist), Terri Vaughn (Lavita Jenkins on The Steve Harvey Show), and many others.

He is civically engaged as well. After the Columbine High School shooting, he founded the

About the Author

National School Safety Advocacy Association. His latest foundations include the Young Entrepreneurship Program (YEP) and the African American Consumer Economic Rights (AACER).

He has authored nine (9) books, *Prayers That Open Heaven, Capturing and Keeping the Pastor's Heart, Powerful Prayers That Open Heaven, Advertising Principles: How to Effectively Reach African Americans in the 21st Century, Discover a New You: A 21 Day Journey to Uncovering Your Uniqueness, From My Heart To Yours: Love Letters From A Loving Father, Today's Apostle: Servants of God, Leading His People towards Unity , Strategic Health Marketing: Marketing Mix and Segmentation Strategies and Daily Quotes for Daily Blessings* .

Dr. Pleasant is the husband of Kimberly Pleasant (whom he loves dearly) and the proud father of three children: Christian, Zion and Nacara.

About the Author

FINI

Made in the USA
Charleston, SC
09 August 2014